Dad Stories

Emily Fontenot

For Josh, Andy, and Gunner—we're alright

CONTENT

Dad Stories

INTRODUCTION

I could pretend this is the first text I've written about you—that would be bullshit. I've written about you in every piece I've ever written. I've written about you in every Barbie scenario I dreamed up. I've written about you in every RPG character I've created. In my writing, I will you into existence. I write the dad I wish you were.

Even in my novel, you exist—I named the dad David for god's sake. But the David there is me. My voice comes through him. I wrote the dad I wanted and needed by making myself the dad to the little girl who is also somehow me (I guess we all write ourselves in various forms and characteristics into characters).

I figured it's time for me to stop recreating you, trying to get you right, showing how many different ways you could have been better. I've spent a lot of time writing the dad who can't get back to his little girl, the Camelot story; the single dad whose life is his daughter; the tragically dead dad whose daughter yearns for him every day, who gets to have an idealized image of him.

Instead, I'm going to write you as you are: mundanely absent while taking up space.

A lot of these feelings started surfacing when Mom was deciding on the divorce. I became a receptacle for her anger. And then I found my own.

Mom says I should talk about it or write about it. She says I need to heal, that I need to forgive you. I don't know if that's what this is. I don't know if that's what I'm trying to get out of this. I don't know if I'm trying to learn more about you or see who you are or feel bad for you. Maybe I'm trying to make you the bad guy. Or maybe I'm still writing you because I'm angry and if I can't have the best dad, I'll make you the worst. You're not the worst. You're not the best.

It was hard to start. I didn't know how to write you, the real you. So, I killed you. I started with a story of myself at your funeral. It's easier to bare all if I could claim it as fiction. It's easier to bare all if you were dead.

The you in these stories is you, Dad. I'm addressing you here because I will never tell you any of this. When I publish this, I will not show you. I won't tell you about it. If you get it, if you read it, I know how you'll respond. You said it in every card for years after the divorce—some iteration of "I know I wasn't the best dad. I'm sorry." Never talking to us about it except for the quick rub of eyes, get 'em nice and red, say sorry.

No examples. No acknowledgement. No changed behavior. I've stopped expecting more from you. This is for me.

LETTING GO

The pulpit is a frightening place. I find myself trembling as I stand surrounded by family members telling stories about you, the rest of the church sitting, staring, tears rolling down their faces, some more loudly than others. Soon it will be my turn, and I haven't decided what to say. What is there to say? What on earth does one say in front of a crowd as foreign and familiar to her as the stars on television about a man that she is not sure she even comprehends though she spent every day of her life knowing him?

I hear Aunt Martha describe you as a five-year-old riding your bike around town with the utmost joy. Suddenly, I have a memory. You taught me how to ride a bike.

You took my training wheels off, and I was terrified. We stood in a face-off—you holding the bike up, waiting for me to get on, me staring at you, resolved not to move until the training wheels were replaced. I was determined, but so were you. I was the defiant child, but a defiant child is not nearly as strong as a man trying to defy his scared self.

Eventually, I got on.

I don't know what you said to get me on that bike, but I got on, shaking. The bike wobbled. I got off. Not even a scrape to prove the terror of a small six-year-old—I assume that's how old I was. But then, I always describe myself as six when I share a memory.

I stood there, still shaking but fighting to control it, hands on my hips, demanding you replace the training wheels.

Another standoff.

You refused to replace the training wheels and demanded I remount the bike. *Stop being scared. There's nothing to be afraid of.*

But I knew. That wobble had shown me that I was right all along. The bike would wobble and I would fall.

And I wasn't going to let that happen again. Instead, I left you with the small, training-wheeless bike and went inside. If you weren't going to put my training wheels back on then I just wouldn't ride. It was as simple as that.

I don't know how you got me back outside, but that's the next thing I remember. I guess you followed me in the house and talked to me some more. I don't remember. All I know is that I made it back outside.

I know you yelled. I remember yelling. *That's enough! Now get on this bike and learn how to ride. You can't be scared of a bike all your life.*

You told me you wouldn't let me fall. You said you wouldn't let go until I was ready. Tentatively, I allowed it.

You warned me you were going to let go before I was ready. I remember. I remember screaming hysterically for you not to let go, but I felt your hands leave the bike. I jumped off. The image of the stubborn child infuriated at the betrayal of her father. You didn't wait for me to say I was ready. You let go amidst my horrified cries.

You had it. Do you really think I would let you fall?

I think of my body decorated by the scars of my clumsy coordination. I can't blame you entirely. The scars are not purely from falling off that bike, but whether you wanted to or not, you had let go of more than just the bike. I had fallen over and over again through the years and gotten up each time. Alone.

Tears stream down my face. It's my turn to say something, but that memory is too personal. It's mine. I cannot share it in front of this crowd, standing over your dead body. I say something else. I don't know what exactly, but I'm sure I said the right thing because as I immersed myself back into the gathering on the pulpit everyone overwhelmed me with physical affection.

And there you are, lying in your coffin, leaving me again.

PRETTY

You were always the one who had to check us out of school or take us to appointments. Your job was flexible like that. Teachers, like Mom, can't just leave in the middle of the day.

Both of you hate being late, so Mom said you should check me out early for my dentist appointment, around 2:45, to avoid after-school traffic. I was excited. I've always liked going to the dentist, and I felt sure I could convince you to get me Sonic either before or after my appointment—probably after. I hadn't brought my toothbrush and you wouldn't want me to embarrass you with a stained mouth. As soon as we got going, you asked if I had brought a toothbrush. When I said no like wasn't it obvious—I was going to the dentist to have my teeth cleaned; we would brush my teeth in the middle of the cleaning—you reached for the pack of Polar Ice sugar-free gum you kept in the door and passed it over, suggesting I chew on it as a substitute. I would wait until after to hint, I decided, though Happy Hour would have made convincing you easier.

We made it through Eunice fine. I don't remember the drive. I assume you were amiable. Did you ask how school was? Was that something you did?

As you turned down the little road to Dr. Duos's office you took a sharp right after the hill. You said nothing as you got out of the truck and left it running. I locked the doors assuming I was meant to stay inside.

You came out minutes later in a huff. I sat quietly and unlocked the doors. You opened yours and took a brush from the yellow bag, crumpling it with the receipt and tucking it into your door. "Come see," you said without looking up.

I was so little then. Third grade feels grown up, but what was I really? Ten? I didn't even fill out the seat and getting down was a three-step process.

I walked to your side of the truck, and you told me to hold my headband. I realized what this was about. Mom fussed that I never brushed my hair, but it killed you. Mom let me put in my headband and go about my day—she had fought with me enough to know it wasn't worth the energy. I turned around.

This was a new brush that I didn't know, and I resented it for being able to know my hair. I resented you for thinking nothing of it. You hadn't even let me pick it out.

You brushed hard, not understanding what length and thickness do to hair. "You know if you would brush it every day it wouldn't get tangled like this," you said as you fought through a knot.

"It's always tangled like this." A fact that you and Mom still choose not to believe.

"Gimme your headband." You reached over my shoulder for it.

I handed it back to you. You put it down on my forehead and pulled it back two or three times, trying to get it perfect. This was not the right technique. It would certainly grab all my hair and I liked some of it to be loose. You pulled the brush through my hair a couple more times for good measure.

"Now," you said, smiling. You handed me the brush. The handle was thick and squishy like the toys at Mr. Gatti's. The handle was blue. I hated blue. "Now you gonna be all pretty for the dentist. Can't go to the doctor like you just got out of bed."

I took the brush home like a prize and made sure everyone knew that it was my brush for my hair and that no one else was allowed to use it. I told Mom you got it for me as a present. I don't know why.

(RE)CONSTRUCTION

Mom wasn't home. Neither were Josh or Gunner. It was just me and Andy, and you.

I was in the fourth grade, so that would put Andy in seventh. It's one of the few memories I have a clear timeline for.

It was a Sunday, so you were inside watching football. Me and Andy were jumping on the trampoline outside. It must have been before Hurricane Rita because I can't imagine it surviving that. I don't think we ever made it through a hurricane without losing a trampoline.

We had moved the basketball goal from the driveway to the side of the trampoline. It had been knocked over in a storm—I don't remember which one—and the rim was bent. I had challenged Andy to a basketball game on the trampoline, and she was beating me terribly. I think the score was something like 60-0. I got so mad as she scored again that I took the basketball and threw it into the yard.

"Let's just jump." Then after about three bounces, I demanded, "Double jump me."

She did and some of my good mood came back as I soared through the air. My pride wouldn't let me show how much fun I was having, so instead I kept yelling at her to bounce me higher.

And she did. We were jumping so aggressively it's no wonder I hurt myself. At one point Andy skyrocketed me so high I think I spent ten seconds in the air. I thought I would never come back down. I remember my stomach dropping while being in the air and desperately wanting to be back on the ground. When my feet finally did hit the trampoline again, my right foot went perpendicular to my leg, folding inward. As if I was a puppet whose master had suddenly dropped the strings, I collapsed.

I just stared at my foot for a while. I had twisted, bruised, and sprained both my ankles enough to know what it felt like and to know that this was not that. I sat there trying to figure out what had just happened, but I couldn't think with Andy's constant jump, jump, jump, and the movement on the trampoline.

"Stop jumping!" I screamed.

"Why? What's wrong?" Andy asked as her jumps became bounces until she was just standing.

I tried to tell her what happened, tried to say, "my ankle," and that's when the tears came. After a few seconds, I yelled, "My ankle!" at her like she should have known.

Andy was fascinated with the medical field at the time and wanted to be a doctor. She sprang into action. "Okay. We have to get you in the house."

"I can't walk," I cried.

She hopped off the trampoline and said, "Wait here. I have an idea."

She came out of the barn wheeling my bike. I just stared at her, dumbfounded.

"Get on," she said.

"I can't walk! How am I supposed to ride my bike?"

She looked at me with the most exasperated scowl a seventh grader can manage and said, "Trust me."

I wiped my face, done with the tears, and scooted off the trampoline. Andy helped me down and got me on my bike. Then she told me to prop my foot up on the handlebars. Of course. I felt so stupid for not realizing that this was her plan. She wheeled me to the front door and helped me up the stairs to the living room, where you sat reclined. She laid me on the couch and propped my foot up with two pillows. She whispered, "I'll be right back." I tried to quiet the leftover sniffles from the crying I had done.

She came back from the kitchen minutes later with supplies. She pressed an ice pack to my ankle and handed me a cup of water and two ibuprofen. "Take that. In a couple of hours I'll give you some more. Make sure you keep the ice where it hurts, and keep it elevated." I took the medicine and nodded at her instructions. "You want some more water?" I nodded, and she left to fill up my cup.

When she came back in the game went to commercial and you asked, "Y'all okay?"

Handing me the water, Andy said, "Yeah, I got it. Don't worry."

And you didn't. You flipped to another game that wasn't on break and turned the volume back up.

That was the first Patriots game I ever watched with you. I think it was the first football game I'd ever really watched. You talked out loud about the team and their work ethic, of Bill Belichick and Tom Brady and Tedy Bruschi, and it felt like you were talking to me. I decided that day that the Patriots were my team too.

Four years later my ankle still hurt so Mom took me to the doctor. A single x-ray showed him that it had fractured in multiple places and had healed wrong. He said it had probably swollen too much for the initial X-rays to show the fractures and that I would have had to get X-rays within the first couple of hours after the accident for them to have seen it. I had to have reconstructive surgery on it.

THE BEAST

Me and Andy tried so hard to be the boys you wanted us to be. Andy was better at it than I was what with the nickname Andy like Andy Griffith, and she was athletic, would hunt or fish with you, she loved riding the four-wheeler—all things that I wasn't or didn't do. She got more time with you too. There were three years between me and her, but only two between me and Gunner—your perfect little boy.

Who was I fooling anyway? I was always the princess, the flower child. I wore lace socks and dresses and fancy clips in my hair. My favorite colors were yellow and pink. I danced instead of walked my way through the world, and the one year y'all got me to play tee-ball, I showed up on picture day with a skirt on that matched my jersey, all my favorite bracelets, a couple rings, and a necklace, hair done with my favorite headband, a pink bat, and lipstick that I had taken from Mom's purse. It was my favorite day of the season.

Then I got older and realized, I guess, that you weren't like the dad from *A Little Princess* and you didn't know how to interact with a fairy daughter, didn't know how to deal with girls at all.

But I tried. I wanted to be a tomboy so bad. In fifth grade I finally got a pair of tennis shoes for school shoes, and I chose the ones with a green and yellow check— John Deere shoes. You liked tractors. Country boys and country tomboys liked tractors. When I was in high school and suddenly Mr. Jeremy didn't like John Deere and swore Case was better, which meant you didn't like John Deere and swore Case was better, I got so mad and didn't know why. You had flipped the script again, and now I had wasted the one pair of shoes I got a year—the one pair we could actually spend money on—on those ugly green and yellow things. That little fifth grader had done everything right. She had tried so hard, and with one comment from a friend, you erased it, made her wrong, again.

Perhaps my biggest failure was football. I watched and understood, learned the rules, picked your team, and knew all the players' names, even posted about it on social media and got into arguments about it at school. But I wasn't a player, so I guess I wasn't enough. Or maybe you couldn't believe that your little ballerina could like what you liked and understand such a masculine game.

You were so rarely present. I don't remember ever playing with you as a kid. I remember playing around you, but never with you. Except for "The Beast." It was this stupid game we made up, or rather, I made up, to insert myself into your and Gunner's playtime. During commercial breaks of Sunday, Monday, and Thursday night football games, we would play.

Gunner would stand next to your recliner, me on the other side of the line, the foot of your recliner. With the little plastic footballs the cheerleaders threw into the stands at Josh's football games, you would recline and "down, set, hut." Gunner would take off for the endzone—the border of the living room area rug—and you would throw the pass. Gunner had to catch it in bounds—so within the area rug—for it to count. Josh was the referee. If Gunner's big toe went even just onto the living room floor, the pass would be ruled incomplete. My job, as the defense, was to prevent Gunner from ever touching the ball. I was taller than him at the time, so it turned into a warped monkey in the middle.

As the ball flew overhead, I would jump and spike it down like a volleyball, then proceed to my victory dance—arms pushed together in front of my stomach, flexing and, in the deepest voice I could manage, cry,

"The Beeeeaaassssstttt!" I would get so excited, and you delighted with my reactions.

But sometimes I wasn't allowed to play because Gunner needed to practice for his real football games. Sometimes though, you tried to coach me.

"Baby, why didn't you intercept that? You could've run it back for your own touchdown."

I chided myself for being so stupid. We hadn't established the rules for my endzone, and I hadn't even considered catching the ball.

I started trying for the interception. I'm not very coordinated so catching the ball proved difficult. My natural reaction continued to be the spike. Once I went for the catch and the ball just grazed the tips of my fingers. Gunner caught it behind me and ran it in for a touchdown. I should've spiked it.

You tried practicing with me a couple of times. Tossing the football straight to me, intended for me to catch, no receiver behind me that I was trying to block. I dropped it almost every time. As if I knew that something significant was on the line, I was anxious and shaking. I couldn't focus on the ball. Instead I watched your face. Eventually you would get annoyed or disappointed and tell me to sit down, that it was GunGun's turn.

One night though, we were playing and after a couple of failed-interceptions-turned-spikes, I caught one. I actually intercepted a pass.

Just as I did though and was about to take off for the end zone, the game came back on. As I tucked the football to start running, you hushed and shooed us. Turning up the TV, you told us, "Alright, that's enough playing. Y'all go sit down."

I didn't even finish running my touchdown. Just dropped the ball on the rug and let it bounce as if I had spiked it. Then I sat in the other recliner parallel to you so I wouldn't get in your way of the TV by going to the couch.

SNAKES AND SUPER BOWLS

The Super Bowl was always a big deal in our family. We usually hosted the party. We would even skip church so you could go to the store to buy meat and make sure everything was ready for when the pre-game shows started at noon. The whole family would come over. We would barbecue and play outside. Blast KBON from a running truck with open doors while the TV in the outdoor kitchen blasted talk shows making predictions and hashing out the season.

Around five o'clock, when it started getting dark, wives and kids would go home to watch the game. Uncles and husbands moved into the outdoor kitchen and settled in for the game.

It was like a rite of passage to be allowed into the outdoor kitchen during the game. By then everyone smelled heavily of beer—even you, with your Coors Cutters—and some, of cigarette smoke. But that was nothing new. Everyone started at noon, at least. None of you ever cooked without a beer—Aunt Viney once told us that when y'all were little and PawPaw would barbecue, it would take all day, and by supper time y'all would ask him when the food would be done. She laughed as she told us he would tell y'all to check the ice chest. His answer was however many beers were left was how much longer it would be.

Me and Andy didn't say anything when we heard the story. We won't speak ill of the dead. But then again, you never spoke ill of him in life either.

I don't remember Josh ever not being allowed to watch the game outside, and I don't remember Andy ever forcing her way in. Before it was me and Gunner's turn—well, before it was Gunner's turn—we would watch the game in the house with Mom. At halftime Mom would go into business mode—rushing us to the bathroom. We knew the drill. There would still be school in the morning, so if we wanted to watch the game to the end, we had to bathe during halftime. I think I was eighteen before I watched a halftime performance.

One night, maybe a Super Bowl night, I had a nightmare, which wasn't unusual. I remembered it—remember it to this day—which was. There are only about three nightmares I remember and mostly the bare bones, but I remember most of this one.

It was Super Bowl night. I was in my PJs, so it would have been after halftime. I must have been young—before I knew to feel shame in PJs, to feel like that was private, before I had to consider bras as necessary things, before the thought of going outside meant I was no longer clean and would have to bathe again, even in a dream. I didn't even put on shoes. I don't remember why I went outside. In real life, it might have been to bring something from the house to you—an errand, sent by Mom. But I remember there being the air of stealth. I might have been sneaking from the house and Mom to you. I might have been sneaking into the outdoor kitchen. Maybe both.

But as I rounded the corner of the house, next to the bent cement post that we leashed Madea and Joe to before y'all gave them away, I noticed how dark it was. None of the outside lights were on, which was odd, especially since we had people over. The only light came through the screen door of the outdoor kitchen. The world was silent except for the din of bugs and the faint sounds of laughter and grown men yelling at the game, talking over each other and to each other about the game, the calls, the plays, the players, the season, other teams, and their memories of playing small-town football.

The walk from the house to the outdoor kitchen felt longer than it ever had and I was suddenly aware of all the spaces of grass and not cement, of the gutters that lined the cement and of all the snakes that could be hiding there. I wanted to transport myself into the sound, be there without the journey. I wanted a flashlight. I wanted you to come outside and get me.

Just then the screen door opened and light spread onto the cement beneath it and the oak tree with our tire swing next to it. It wasn't you that stepped out but Uncle Roland. Round, jovial Uncle Roland. He would help me, I remembered thinking. But before he could see me, I saw a dark shape in the flood of light. It was an anaconda, huge and black, and it lunged for Uncle Roland. I couldn't do anything. I stood frozen as his hands flew up to his face—the two missing fingers silhouetted by the light behind him. He had lost them as a kid when they were run over by a tractor. My brain still can't process how it happened, having touched many tractor tires and felt all their deep grooves. Since I was a kid, I've run the close-up of the accident through my mind, trying to make sense of it. Uncle Roland hadn't cried out and the sounds from beyond the lit door continued uninterrupted.

Then I saw you. You hadn't been inside with everyone else. You stepped out from behind the outdoor kitchen with a shotgun. You aimed for the anaconda, and I woke up.

BURIED BY THE BARN

Growing up, Gunner and I always had birthday parties together. We were close in age and both our birthdays were in the summer. Plus it was cheaper to throw one party instead of two. Mostly we opted for water themes—slip 'n slides and pools and inflatable water slides. After we hit middle school though, the Skating Rink was the clear choice. Much cooler, we deemed.

I don't remember you ever being at those—and they were Gunner's too. So maybe it wasn't just me, wasn't just the girls. Maybe it just depended on your own interests.

At our last skating party, I was too old not to know how to skate. Mrs. Debbie laughed and jokingly held my belt loops and walked me around the rink. It didn't help. I still can't roller skate.

After the party, we went home to you. You were boiling crawfish for us in the outdoor kitchen—the screened-in part. We barely used that part. Gunner didn't even like crawfish. You offered to peel them for him, but he refused. You fried shrimp for him instead. The sky was dark, not raining yet but close.

You asked how the party was and without waiting for a response told us the crawfish should just be a few more minutes.

It wasn't long after that. We heard the screech of brakes. You jumped up—you had been facing the windows that showed the front yard and highway. Ricky had been hit and killed by that car. I don't remember whether we buried him before or after we ate. I can't imagine us leaving his lifeless body out there while we ate, but then, how could we eat after? The weird part about death is that life goes on. Your stomach will still grumble, reminding you that cake is not a meal, even though your dog won't wait at your feet while you eat this time. Things will still be funny. You will still laugh, and you will still sleep.

We got another Cocker Spaniel not long after that. We named Ricky Two. He got hit by a car too—Ricky Too.

You buried him before telling us. Sometimes I wonder if you actually buried any of them, or if you just chucked them over the levy and into a field to be used as fertilizer. You never cried—I remember that. You would just walk in, wring your hands, frown, and look down. The bad news always started with "Hey, guys…"

Sometimes I think it was Mom who told you to tell us you buried them. Did it make you sad to see us cry over them?

I know I asked you where you buried them more than once. I don't remember really being told. "By the side of the barn" comes to mind, but then again, you knew—or should have known—that I was never brave enough to walk there. There were too many snakes. Maybe you really did bury them there. Maybe it was convenient.

We never had another skating party. We never had crawfish for our birthday again either. They were out of season by summer anyway.

MOM FUCKED US WITH WEIGHT SHIT

Both legs in. Stop at the thigh. Breathe. Jump. Jump again. Jump until they pull past my thighs and my Big. Fat. Ass. Until I feel fabric touch my hips. Then jump one more time, cursing the low-rise trend as I force them over my love handles. Tug until it feels like the jeans are up my fucking vagina. I've never even used a tampon, yet somehow I endure this every time I wear jeans.

Once they're in place, stop again. Pray that they'll still button, that the zipper will stay up. Remind myself that I was on my period last week and that's why they were painfully tight. Promise myself that this week I'll start, start over, start again. This time I'll lose the weight. Suck in, hard. Button. Zip. Hold my breath: three, two, one. Slowly exhale—don't scare the zipper with the extra pressure of oxygen. Breathe.

Give them ten minutes. They'll stretch out. Then I'll be able to move, to breathe. That's just how jeans work.

"We're leaving in five minutes," Mom calls to the house, accusatorily, like it wasn't like this every Sunday.

The zipper held. I'll have to speed things up. Stretch a little. Bend. Help the fabric loosen. Wonder if they've been shrinking in the dryer. Remind myself to start hanging them to dry. Breathe again and walk out of my room, at least fix some cereal before y'all corral us out.

You, in the kitchen with a water from your ice chest. We didn't drink bottled water in the house—it was a waste of money. You wipe the dew with a paper towel, ease the bottle into a huggie. It's brown, subtle, the Logan Fournerat Cattle Company one. Smile. Walk past to the pantry. Grab a box of cereal.

"The car's already running." You never were a breakfast person.

"I'll fix it in a cup. Take it with us."

Gather cup and spoon. Pour cereal, milk. Walk over to the island. Drop spoon. Great. Jeans aren't stretched out yet. Bend slowly, at the waist—not the knees—to pick it up.

"Bend your knees." Your voice is suddenly harsh, angry.

Three things go through my mind one right after the other:

Red. Hot. Everywhere. Not anger. A flush. Embarrassment.

Was it that easy to tell? They fit. They buttoned, zipped then stayed. I had looked in the mirror. They fit. I'm a size six.

You couldn't tell. And if you could? What was it to you? Couldn't you let me handle it? They would stretch out. I would lose the weight. And since when did you care? Since when did you even see me? We let you have your denial. We let you believe all sorts of things: That your brother's ███████. That your dad wasn't ██ ████████. That your sister didn't ████████ ████████. That she had ████████████████ ████████████. Or better yet, that she hadn't had to. Because it had never happened. That she hadn't ████████████████████.

They fit.

Did you think I was trying to be sexy? Mom said all guys ever thought about was sex. Did you think that's what this was? Practice? Me? More red, flushed. Can you imagine? I can promise you, that's not what this was. I could just see, feel every seam bursting if I bent at the knees, breaking the wooden planks locking them in place. They needed time to stretch out.

And now my cereal was soggy. Throw it out. Go to the car, silent.

I don't know if I'll ever forgive you for that.

EMERGENCY CONTACT

If I was sick at school, Mrs. Patsy called you. This was still true after I started my period. It was easier for you to come get me or bring me a change of clothes than Mom. You never complained about it—you always seemed happy to do it.

Usually, you just brought me another pair of school shorts, but there had been a mix-up once where you brought me a pair of Andy's which were much too big at the time. I remember being proud of how tight I had to pull the belt to keep them up but also not understanding how you couldn't tell the difference between my side of the closet and Andy's. Within two years I would be wearing Andy's old school clothes while she was away at Northwestern State. I never told you that you messed up, but I did tell Mom. She must've told you because the next time I had to call you, you checked me out of school so I could change at home.

I was silent as I got in your truck, the jacket around my waist, feeling like a child with a soiled diaper. You

41

drove toward town instead of home and asked, "What happened?" You didn't take your eyes off the road. "Were you not prepared or...?" You trailed off, waiting for me to fill in the blanks.

I remember feeling so uncomfortable at having to answer that, at having to have that conversation. I was embarrassed at having to explain myself, as any girl would be, but I also remember feeling proud—happy? thankful?—that you asked, that you weren't treating this like a scared little boy who couldn't stand the thought of a period.

"I was—I—it just happened," I answered.

You nodded as if that explained it.

You stopped at Dollar General and asked if I wanted anything or needed supplies. I didn't, but I did ask for a Dr. Pepper.

When you came back to the truck, you handed me a coke with a small box of generic Midol. "The lady at the counter said this helps with cramps and stuff," you said.

I thanked you and took the box. What I didn't tell you was that I couldn't take those pills. I do cramp a lot, and they would undoubtedly help. But the way they help is the problem. Midol and other medicines like it, like headache medicine and Tylenol, thin the blood, make the uterus easier to scrape. You get fewer clots and more free-flowing blood. The last thing a girl like me with a heavy flow needs is thinner blood. I'd take the clots with the cramps all day.

I still have that same container of medicine. I might have taken three doses since you bought them for me all those years ago. They're long expired by now. I keep them in my car.

TRASH

I drove home and back to Lafayette after my last day of the summer semester. I had to pick up Matt who was low on cash and couldn't afford the gas. I needed a friend—I did for a while—to facilitate my rebellion.

I got my nose pierced then went to Port Barre to hang out with church friends. I'd hoped we would go late, and we did. I got to come home to a sleeping house. My face was safe for the night, and I could enjoy it.

I had to clean the piercing though—probably should have hours earlier but it never got infected so no harm, no foul. I got out Mom's gumbo mug—the green one Gunner painted "I ♥ Mom" on in gold at church—filled it with hot water and salt, then shoved my face in it, making sure my right nostril was submerged. Watching the clock. Making bubbles. Giggling at myself.

I heard y'all's bedroom door open, kitchen side, my left. The free side of my face lit by the oven hood light.

"Hey, baby," Mom whispered groggily. I lifted my face from the mug and smiled in profile. "Did you have fun?"

"Yeah, we did."

"Good. I'm going back to bed, little one. I just wanted to tell you goodnight." She paused for a second. "Gimme a hug." And I did, awkwardly, keeping the right side of my face from her. If she noticed that or the mug of saltwater, she didn't mention it. She must not have wiped the sleep from her eyes.

The next morning I woke up and smiled in the mirror at the tiny glint of the stud. Then I breathed and navigated the kitchen, all odd angles and half glances as I passed Mom on my way to the coffee pot.

Andy was in my usual spot so I had to take the seat on the couch that would put my right nostril on display for everyone to see. Andy noticed first. Little snitch. She had noticed my tattoo first too. "Is that—are you serious? How trashy." She was never one for subtlety. I glared at her over my coffee.

"What?" Mom called from the kitchen, and seeing the standoff going on between us, looked to me and said, "Emily Reece. What did you do?"

I slipped on my best, most innocent and awkward smile, and tilted the right side of my face toward her. "I got my nose pierced."

I half expected her to walk over, grab my chin, and inspect it, like in the movies, but she didn't. She just sighed. "I hope you've thought about this. Can you even have that for work?"

"I can take it out if I need to."

"Yeah and when you decide you don't want it anymore, it's gonna look like a big blackhead on your face for the rest of your life," Andy chimed in.

"Look. Who cares? I like it. I've wanted one for a long time."

"You know what? Fine." Mom threw the dish towel down. "But you have to tell your dad."

I looked her in the eyes and said okay much more confidently than I felt. Andy snickered in *my* chair.

Timing and grace are things that I obviously didn't learn from Mom. As soon as you walked in, she cocked her head at me, expectantly. I motioned a quick "chill," but she was going to wait me out.

You noticed the tension, which is really saying something, considering. "What?" you asked Mom.

"Ask Emily what she did last night." Arms crossed. Eyes never taken from mine.

You turned to me.

"Well?"

I broke from Mom's stare. I was scared my voice would crack if I tried to say it, so I tilted my face again, Vanna Whited my nose, and smiled.

You did that thing where you lean closer and squint as if you could see any better while you were still across the room from me. "What's that?" you asked.

"She got her nose pierced," Mom answered for me—a small victory. Patience is a virtue.

"It's so trashy," Andy added.

You straightened. "I think it's cute. You know it's in fashion now. A lot of girls around the office have them. I like it." As you said all this, you had noticed the TV, the Kardashians a regular Saturday morning feature, and crossed the room to your chair. You held out your hand to Andy for the remote. "Gimme dat. There's got to be something better to watch."

THE TALK

You were home and intent on talking to us.

"Girls," you started, the way you always did when talking to us about anything remotely important. You stood by the stove and asked us to sit. We did. Almost immediately you scrunched up your face like you were holding back tears. I'm usually pretty good at hiding my emotions, but I'm sure I must have cocked my eyebrow.

I was relieved though. You were finally going to tell us about the divorce. Andy and I wouldn't have to walk around like Mom hadn't already told us, hadn't been discussing it with us for months.

I don't remember most of the conversation. I remember almost nothing you said. I remember being angry though. Being angry at you and your manipulation of the truth, at Andy for crying and giving you the sympathy you wanted, at knowing she would say she wasn't really crying and knowing she'd be lying.

You said you were leaving Mom. You said you "just couldn't take it anymore." You didn't mention that you had started drinking again or that you'd called Mom drunk from a work site a couple times, that her decision was finalized when you showed up at home—me, Andy, and Gunner asleep in our room—drunk and stumbling. After nearly twenty years, I'll never understand how quickly you shifted back into that life. It still makes me angry how open you are about it now.

You told us you would always love us. I didn't know that was up for grabs in divorce allocations.

You told us if we ever needed anything to call you. Like an ex who wants to stay friends.

You said you hoped we'd come visit you. Like you were going to prison and we would have to schedule visits.

I almost laughed. I study language. I knew what that meant—you wouldn't reach out to us. We would have to visit you. Andy said, "Of course." I blinked.

My head throbbed and screamed without language the whole time you spoke. When you fake-cried I wanted to throw things at you, anything within reach. My mind played reels of alternate realities. I sat.

I wanted to laugh and scream that I had told Mom to leave you, that I told her she owed it to us—to her girls—to leave, to teach by doing how we shouldn't just accept behavior.

I sat quietly.

You hugged us after, and then you left. Maybe you just went outside to sit. Or maybe you went cut the grass. Maybe you had already moved out. I don't remember.

THANKS FOR THE GESTURE

You didn't text me until after you left the driveway. Your truck never stopped running. I was awake. I heard you. I lied. I didn't wake up too late after getting your text, I heard you knock. I let the dogs bark.

I was still in bed though. I didn't have a bra on. Those are the easy excuses. Honestly, I just didn't want to see you. You weren't there to see me anyway. You were snooping, as you do. Digging through the shit in the carport, wishing Mom was home, wondering where she was, and I didn't want to explain. Didn't want to tell you she was with her boyfriend. Didn't want to lie and tell you she was somewhere else.

I don't even drink coffee anymore, but you wouldn't know. Why would you?

I forced myself back to sleep so it would seem honest when I woke up hours later and texted you apologizing. Apologizing after I cried because you came and I didn't want to see you. Apologizing because I knew if I let you in the house you would ask to use the bathroom and move past mine into Mom's and you

51

would dig through her drawers, and then I would have to apologize to Mom for letting you.

I didn't go right outside, I waited. Got dressed. Ate breakfast. Took a deep breath and opened the door. Two cups on the patio table. They were cold. I threw them away.

REACHING OUT

Waiting for someone to die is hard. Imagine waiting, to die. Watching is bad enough.

It's mostly watching. Not the face because that tells nothing. MawMaw Betty—your mom—sleeps mostly, wakes when we rouse her because another family member's shown up to say goodbye. Her sleeping face looks like I imagine mine did when I was six and pretending to die while playing Power Rangers with Gunner or trying to scare Opie and Lucy, the dogs that were with us the longest.

Instead, watch the chest. Is it rising? Falling? Watch the toes for any tiny twitch. But while watching, remember that when snakes and bugs die, they keep twitching even if they're cut into several different pieces. I think of that for a while. Then I remind myself how horrible I am to look at her and think of a snake cut into several pieces to make sure, but at least it reminds me of stories and laughter we had as a family, back when we used to all spend time together, and she would like that. Right?

I wonder: Is it hard to die with so many faces watching? Does she notice? Does it feel like a lot of pressure? To die sooner and not keep everyone waiting? To hold off and make sure everyone can say she stayed strong? Like when PawPaw was dying and they said he stayed alive just long enough to see my padan arrive—later than his kids because he lives in Texas and had to drive.

Is that strong? Or is it just painful?

Her breaths come harder now. They don't rise and fall easily like when I used to pretend to be asleep on the couch so you would carry me to bed. They rise slowly and slump out hard. It looks painful.

And what do I do when I need to pee but her breaths come like that? For those final moments, people only tell stories about where they were. Who she waited for to die. To go to the bathroom and what? Miss the last cinematic breath? Come out, hands washed, knowing everyone probably heard you pee, and what? Everyone's crying? Stopped crying? Are just still and you break that perfect stillness, hands still damp?

Mom is in the car, not wanting to intrude. She had come in and said goodbye, exchanged niceties. She's probably crying, mourning it all—the death of the woman who loved her and her son so much that she married that woman's son just to be part of the family and that, because she finally made the decision to leave him, she couldn't be there with that woman while she died.

But you were on your way in from a job in Texas and she didn't want anything to get in between you and your mom.

When you walk in, you go straight to her side. Everyone clears a path for you, like it was somehow known that this moment would be most important for you when only a moment earlier Dawn was laughing that there was no way "Uncle David would sleep there. He would go to his house and *his bed*."

That was the first time since the divorce that your eyes didn't find your kids' first or move toward us without regard for the space around you. You didn't seem like Dad in that moment. You were just a son, saying goodbye to your mom and not understanding how or why or what that meant.

She died the day I got back to Illinois. I had to leave for orientation, for the sake of my assistantship. I didn't get to go to her funeral.

The day after the funeral, Mom called and asked if I had heard from you. I hadn't. I understood being distant during these times. She told me I should reach out. That you shouldn't have to call or text for me to put in the effort. She said I should call you.

I texted you. "Hey, Paw. How you holding up?"

ABOUT THE AUTHOR

Emily Fontenot is a writer from south Louisiana. Her first book, *Hurricanes, Cypress Trees, and Other Synonyms for Home*, was published by Press 254 in December 2022. She is the Visiting Assistant Professor of Creative Writing at Millikin University in Illinois. An excerpt from her novel-in-progress is now available in *South 85 Journal*, where it was nominated for the 2022 Best of the Net Anthology. Her fiction has also been published in *Quail Bell Magazine*, *Gone Lawn*, *The Southwestern Review*, and others. Her creative nonfiction has appeared in *Children, Churches and Daddies* and their subsequent home press collections and *Hive Avenue Literary Journal*.

ABOUT THE PRESS

Unsolicited Press is based out of Portland, Oregon and focuses on the works of the unsung and underrepresented. As a womxn–owned, all–volunteer small publisher that doesn't worry about profits as much as championing exceptional literature, we have the privilege of partnering with authors skirting the fringes of the lit world. We've worked with emerging and award–winning authors such as Savannah Cooper, Amy Shimshon–Santo, Brook Bhagat, Elisa Carlsen, and Rosalia Scalia.

Learn more at Unsolicitedpress.com. Find us on Twitter and Instagram at @UnsolicitedP.